Verse X Life Growth

OrangeBooks Publication

1st Floor, Rajhans Arcade, Mall Road, Kohka, Bhilai, Chhattisgarh 490020

Website: **www.orangebooks.in**

First Edition, 2023

VERSE X LIFE *Growth*

A COLLECTION OF VERSES

KUSUM CHOUDHARY

OrangeBooks Publication

www.orangebooks.in

What is Life?

We think life is miserable; sometimes it's joyful, hurting, beautiful, struggling, bad suffering, or karma? Just like our moods.

We think our life is miserable at times, we feel it's hurting, and we don't want it.

Did we ever think it could be beautiful if we start moving out exploring what's at the deepest core of the earth or maybe just in our day-to-day?

Poems are part of life; they're like the voice of the people who can't explain themselves. Many times, poems are about non-living, conveying feelings in their voices through verse. I could say that life is a book filled with different turns just like different poems/quotes.

As a poet, writing a poem daily can be a powerful practice for personal growth. Each day presents a new opportunity to explore your innermost thoughts and feelings and to express them in a creative and meaningful way. By committing to this daily practice, you may find that you become more in tune with your emotions and surroundings, and that your writing becomes richer and more nuanced over time.

Similar to writing, you get used to understanding nature as well as things around you differently in the newest form. There would have been a point in life where you get stuck in a decision. Probably, you don't understand yourself.

The poems I've written in upcoming pages describe how they affect you when writing daily as a writer and explode your mind with different and various extraordinary ideas.

As a poet, understanding one's feelings through a poem is like exaggerating oneself.

Growth: It's important to remember that growth is a process, and it takes time and effort to achieve. But when you commit to making small improvements each day, the results can be truly transformative. Whether it's through writing, reading, exploring, or simply being present at the moment, there are countless ways to embrace the journey of self-improvement.

I've seen people in my life find it difficult to put themselves into words.

Life is like a narrow valley among enormous mountains; sometimes, it's suffocating, and sometimes, it's a slow process.

Index

Day 1
Flames

I was calm as an ocean,

Without a breeze!

With words, he thought,

Tried to seize!

I'm vast; he's just a stone.

Burned flowers with his flame,

Falling petals felt like a broken gem!

- Kusum Choudhary

Day 2
Be You

You don't have to harm yourself just to fit in,

It's okay not to be accepted by people around you,

Stay as you are, live as you want,

Try making your life worth living, not because you got it,

But because you own it,

You are a part of the divine/sacred Tree,

Just because you feel you're excluded, that doesn't mean GOD does not include you!

- Kusum Choudhary

Day 3

Your mind is like a greedy bird,

But it does not let you choose the right word,

Your heart is like a sensitive worm,

But it does not let you easily accept to learn.

Your eyes are like a fragile leaf,

But it does not let you stop the unwanted tears.

Nature supports us by being our biggest pillar,

Our disapproval in our thoughts plays the role of Being the biggest killer.

Feel the presence of nature,

Decline the thought that do not believe in beautiful creatures!

- Kusum Choudhary

Day 4
Wounded Butterfly

I'm grateful to be born,

Daylight and moonlight are way too long

*Drudgery work I do, ain't frightened the way
I'll get torn.*

Span short don't even know where I belong;

Tongue-tied, tiny elusive,

Aided others I'm lost in the area of delusive,

The scale of as dreamy colors,

Fragile me, combined distinctive marking said rumors.

- Kusum Choudhary

Day 5

Your days or maybe months might not be going in the way you expect them to go,

Let yourself know confidently empty passing of your days/months will not threaten your life,

Until and unless your soul is ready to accept uneasiness of those empty days going...

Can be made worthy,

Let your heart and mind be at rest,

Sometimes, that's the preparation for the upcoming best.

Remember, you will not always be in that depressed and tired condition;

The most unbearable days prepare for the most joyful and unexpected change.

That's a small part of the universe's indication!

- Kusum Choudhary

Day 6
Choose Your
Do We or Please do

We don't live to fulfill people's expectations, do we?

Take a moment to be grateful for receiving an unthreatening life, please do!

We don't sweat and work hard just to get accepted by society, do we?

Take a moment and praise the Supreme Being for continuous functioning work; please do!

We don't enjoy this busy world because we're too busy to bet the race, do we?

Take a moment and gaze at night to know.

There's another world without competition made for just to be yourself; please do!

We don't see the trap of manipulative people, do we?

Take a moment and smile that you're too kind to
understand such traps; please do!

We don't see miracles, do we?

Take a moment; catch the helping hand of nature you'll
keep glaring at the beauty of miracles: please do!

We don't consider people without any benefit, do we?

Take a moment to believe in a soul that works for little
smirk of others: please do!

- Kusum Choudhary

Day 7

Moments define your past,

But don't carve your future,

Movements make your future,

Life is filled only with disturbances that will always be a rumour,

Your earnings might be marked, legally…

Your kind gestures are remarked preciously.

What you achieve is up to you,

Because your act of generosity was always new!

Every turn takes you somewhere you need to be there,

Rare happenings shouldn't be examined as unfair!

- Kusum Choudhary

Day 8

The unchosen paths are difficult when chosen by rare,

*Don't put your mind in thought that
life is easy and unfair...*

His roads are clear with invisible hurdles;

*Belief and unquestioning of yours,
wipes a lot of burdens.*

Opening an eye at an unfamiliar place,

*Chances are wonderful,
because you're chosen for beautiful places to gaze!*

Leaving at a time to reach somewhere,

Graving your feet takes you nowhere!

- Kusum Choudhary

Day 9

Prepared plans, destroys unexpected surprises;

Unremarkable days,
noticeable hurdles are puzzling for life crises!

You are alive wherever you are,

Eyes that'd lived a moment raised their presence that
far.

Enormous the beauty of your character rays,

The day-born act lets you live a lively act of joy
when at silence, as it's the part that plays!

- Kusum Choudhary

Day 10

Floral's sweetness is a perfect bliss;

Roaming fearless once, they'll miss it!

*Ambiance of mahogany tree in absence of noisy
talkful creatures;*

The uplifting scent of sandalwood;

Defames the bible as greener with green,

*A bunch of safflowers showers the pureness of
life as respawn;*

A rose filled with gold empowers you as shining dawn.

Tilting of leaves as a pause in daily life,

*Over days of worthless mud as a pathetic
work is a wasteful drive!*

- *Kusum Choudhary*

Day 11

You don't have to wait for the right time to arrive,

Make things a lot easier when done before thrive.

Sore thoughts affect a point in,

The personality you spread as an aura of you,

Cannot be owned by you of yours few.

Once a chance to show,

The elegant turning, lies of flames burning,

Yours that'd be a return glow,

In the end, the sense of chaos is gonna blow!

- Kusum Choudhary

Day 12

You chose to be kind and spreaded it up,
Gentle cold breeze took your inner sore and faded it,

Never got found in explored crowd,
Tireless years you spent made you once proud.

An unimaginable miracle you feel when on the urge to rest,

Markable the battle you had,

Lead procrastination of your realization made you the BEST!

- Kusum Choudhary

Day 13

You gain a pearl after all those undergone work,
I call it a 'SKILL';

Many ways, action for one. I call it 'GOAL'.

Filled with elements, invisible as air; I call it 'SOUL'.

Overflowing out of a boundary, still clear as salt;
I call it 'TEARS'.

Unacceptable phobia of unusual, dark as night;
I call it 'FEAR'.

Release to prison of pain, genuine as scent of lilies;
I call it 'LAUGHTER OF SMILES'!

More....

- Kusum Choudhary

Day 14

Rains of tears can be converted to rains of GLORY,

*Lightning of anger can be converted into
lightning of TOLERANCE,*

*Heavy storm of chaos can be converted into
a heavy storm of mindfulness,*

*Uneasy wind of awful behavior can be converted into
uneasy wind of superior guider,*

*The nature of departed soul can be converted into
nature of healing LEADER,*

*Darkness of the cloud in mind can be converted into the
rise after dark of the cloud in HOPE!*

- Kusum Choudhary

Day 15

Cure the pain with pain,

Remove your burden with rain!

Move yourself like a river in flow,

Without letting your glow go,

Be amazed by your presence,

Try thinking world with your absence.

Load for others, but don't cut your own feathers
Here life is like season-changing-weathers!

Wipe your tears of the hardships that'd you bear,
Set your smiles of achievement that'd take you miles.

Rise your personality of bright that'd made
you sunshine!

- Kusum Choudhary

Day 16

Purchase the joy that you couldn't chase,

Sell the comfort not just because self couldn't get it,

Avail the glory that words couldn't tell your story,

Make it alone without people;
you couldn't get with people

Just,

Leave incomplete behind,

Forget to blame,

Place your site of yours to your main AIM,

Swallow the lies, know truth never dies.

Attain the clam when disappears,

Detach anger when feared.

Voices of invisible in your head,

Burn it with the fragrance of faith!

- Kusum Choudhary

Day 17

Bare the failures of your efforts,

It's okay when your heart can't accept that dirt.

Enhance the grip that owns your power,

Be at your soft era that blooms like a sunflower.

Wouldn't mind if you fall when it's for REVOLUTION,

Adore it with embrace to let itself raise,

Growth is what I call EVOLUTION.

Backing a step for pause;
Won't harm you any bit of cause.

To learn, how busy the world is,
Live in delusion for money.

An art to convey magic in words,
Still lacks the spark of holy nature's LOVE!

- Kusum Choudhary

Day 18

Break the height which stops you from growing,

Be a river that never stops flowing,

Own a spark like a star that never stops glowing,

Attain a chill relief that never stops blowing,

Generate a curiosity like a kid to learn
that never stops knowing,

Superior for self, inferior for god be
that you never stops bowing,

Don't sink in when you're meant that you never
stop floating,

Have a heart that isn't very harsh to accept, not expect
from the aspect of easy-going!

— **Kusum Choudhary**

Day 19

Switch on the light which is keeping you in dark,

Head on the track, which is filled with foot cracks,

Walls can be knocked when ways of demise are crossed.

Fears burned when flames of fire tore,

Stuck of an eye reversed roles of people into game,

Rhythm of life in a pseudo attempt to bring their name.

Scenarios get random thoughts,

Truth folds when reality is really taughts!

- Kusum Choudhary

Day 20

Aloud is the scream of success,

Silence is the pain of failures.

Coldness in the discipline is to achieve,

Patience in consistency is to receive.

Running of time, exactly how far is time running?

To catch a missed train how did you really miss the on-time train?

Lost in the world; exactly where's this world made you lost.

Shoulder of sore, endure it with cure.

Precisely, does it truly impact in world of huge?

*Reliance on an event exactly how far does
that let you make?*

*Unfinished business kept on seeing exactly completed
effort how long you've been?*

- Kusum Choudhary

Day 21
Morning Cold

Ears bliss with the music of the flute,
The shiny sky turned into foggy blue.

Missing of an irritation of noise, glad
It's morning cold with birds' choice,

Sleep of all, talk of floral with folk.
Get hurried at usual time until
He waits for another dawn.

Awakening of spiritual guide ain't internally;
From house bell's prayers, which are externally.

A time of 9 of the night might be a sight,
Windy breeze with comfy shawl,
Until we all get the morning cold again!

- Kusum Choudhary

Day 22
A Traumatized Life Yet Good With Gods' Belief

Hesitate a moment, which kills a seed growth;
Wave a hand of the end for the lead role.

Break a glass if fineness bothers,
Rather than seeing a lot with sealed tongue,
Cause of grief may be loss of a leaf,
Get a laugh to go, the lot has a relevant brief.

A mirror of blurry image, similar
Seeing your face in wavy water of waves.

Might be a road with endless Fog and grave!

Grunting breath with stopless chase for better self-gain,

Even in the darkness of rain,
I'll be the sunshine in the midst of rain.

Away without talk of a curse,

I'll be the clearer of my pain!

- Kusum Choudhary

Day 23
A Purpose

A reminder to wake in cause alarm,

Take a move to remove a day,

Might yours be the worst?

Could you not even say anyone, HEY?

Business handle by themselves,
It's for cause of stone step.

Miles's feet are firm to climb,

Might yours be unchosen road,

Could you not even give anyone a smile?

I maybe someone for them or a backbone of my own,

Getting everything together by me for me,

Could they not even pat my head, just cause, I'm he?

Rose my hands, clap for my own pull-off,

Might be all on different paths.

Could they not even be,

Someone else to be proud of?

Throw it off as if forever gone,

Be glad of acceptance that you came and made for,

Might be separated, still

Could you not even accept ignorance for its own ignore?

- Kusum Choudhary

Day 24
I Wish

Unseen cries die in the seen past,

Couldn't believe I've gotten another day as vast,

Everyone to each other merely sees as a prop,

Wish, if all I had, to lead,

Like to shape a tree, I'd crop!

Yet, now and then, or else never,

I'd wish to learn not to turn life this bad ever;

A dried sentence turned in never stopping regret,

Climbed wall fell in seconds,

Blink an eye missed colorful light,

Just because on a big day, forgot and slept overnight!

A mistake is of learning,

A regret is of vein burning!

Glare at an empty sky, zooming beyond the sky,

Wait for spring, and you'd see me once free for last,
I'll fly.

Major in minor for unique, I notice,

I'd leave it as sugar in bitter,

Staying in won't make sweeter than sweet,

Oh my, it's just what I wish?

- Kusum Choudhary

Day 25
The Sunset

More alive when actually wanna stay absent,

A sunset does bring worth,

During the counting of your presence!

Dullness across face and relief of washing over your stress,

Forever gone when eyes meet another ray of beautiful sunsets;

Noise in every corner, away from beaches

Heartfelt, when everything sinks,

It's the only top that the sun reaches!

Mighty lights of colorful rays,

Crumbled the joyful heart,

The goodbye when every

Sunset says!

Unaccompanied any wall in part of the world,

Yet, missed a lot because it was the day of rain;

Teary eyes hear, it could have been different,

Here I'm craving the sunset once again!

- Kusum Choudhary

Day 26
Appearing Dark

It's 4am; silence roams around streets and households,

*Not present people or emptiness of noise makes
it feel colder;*

Sometimes, a pureness of soul drips in,

Through their night tears,

*When their simplicity moves like them in,
corners every near!*

Lighten your own aura as northern lights,

Authentic jubilant seek to recreate,

Is there any season, you left

Remain to celebrate?

Crowd in daylight seems for one's purpose

Sudden disappearance starts to say
IT'S APPEARING DARK!

- Kusum Choudhary

Day 27
Words of Eyes

Unvisited space once left after seen,

Screams, to look back and stay

Did you hear without the words?

Moving onto subsequent places

Ever starred of looking in

Left behind with long gazes

Did you hear something in absence of words?

Visit, light among two,

Have you counted words from hearing?

Or

Did you leave unseen when words were spoken by eyes?

Sharp the power mind trained,

Leaving its weak

Happened to get a command,

Did you look at tension passed through words of eyes!

- Kusum Choudhary

Day 28
Force of Mind

Freaks out the anxiety that kills,

Pierce it thoroughly, but never heals;

Lives without any connection,

Gets lost, demanding to achieve that DISTINCTION,

Thoughts running like the horse in a race,

LOSES its will could get superior in any case.

Sits with absence, Spaced out in its thought gaze,

HEALS with god's presence; reality checks
his midst range.

Reckless his body, strings messed like mixed threads,

Encourages his livelihood; joins battle of race,

Shows the love how elegantly he SPREADS!

- Kusum Choudhary

Day 29
Mind's Eye

A MIRACLE turned into mixtures,

Only meant to be felt by creatures!

Droplets of RAIN on her cheeks,

Reminds her of her first MEET!

Its presence made everything around PLEASANT,

HIS absence created every little thing unpleasant!

GENTLE blow filled with a flow of petals,

IN RAIN,

Long years away, built a heart of a METAL

IN PAIN!

RAINS showering its burn,

DRAINS her affection for his long-lost LOVE!

Keeps behind its mark,

Still, shines BRIGHTER like glitters at night,
as a SPARK!

- Kusum Choudhary

Day 30
Didn't Want Still Got

The world is too noisy,

When you're used to a peaceful room.

Events are jumbled with different opinions,

When you're used to listening like a child.

Meaningless words from strangers seem boring,

When you're used to continuing with sharp working.

Considerable amounts of public behavior as average,

When you're used to being a guide as a leader.

Judgmental minds hold on to causing trouble,

When you're used to speaking as a humble!

- Kusum Choudhary

Day 31
Street Walk at 7pm

*Mind was filled with chaos still trying to write
poem to solve chaos.*

Traffic of different ideas ended up with just a long walk,

Spends hours sitting,

Dreaming stairs towards star reaching;

Different glow of various lamp lights,

Falling leaves yet the comforting winter hits,

It's feels right.

Touches of laughter and warmth of people besides,

How will it bring smiles near streets it's
when the winter decides;

The sooner sun goes down,

Growth of fog makes its appearance,

At the same time, MOON decides to go up,

Slow of people walk in disappears streets begin
its silence!

- Kusum Choudhary

Day 32
An Empty Stomach

Dreaming aloud to be full and be fortunate,

Compared to yesterday, yet every day grateful for today.

Bathe in a cave for search and ended up losing each grip,

Dizzy morning with a little growl,

Hunger builds with a will make you crawl.

Game of day-to-day thought for earn or let the inner system burn?

Tracking the weekly rule yet messed up and missed what owned.

Under condition of lively death never stoned,

The ay of every turn doesn't end.

An empty stomach of food isn't always intended!

- Kusum Choudhary

Day 33
Fly in Honor of Bird

Beyond the sky, there is a place reserved for each,

One and only the eyes see sharp like a tip.

Clashing of clouds when wings pass

A ray shines on stones which got hammered

Shoulders loaded with burden formed dews
crossing beyond.

Gentle peace owned you one day a throne

Wars with wild sliced every edge of fighting bone!

Reaching false people puts step away
from your own home;

Ain't nobody an eagle might be a crow clone?

The back that flew high made you outgrown it!

- Kusum Choudhary

Day 34
A Taste of Life

The bitterness is decreasing with the bitter I'm drinking,

*The lies are getting swallowed, and truths
are getting folded.*

Eyes are manipulated to get into loops that are held,

*Breaks a miserable change that could've stared into
others' souls.*

Paints the painting dark without the color black,

*Ain't people know it's built from many different beautiful
cracks!*

Maybe it's scenery of the sunset hiding the burn,

Caused from uneven still stable because of effort,

Stepped onto the land of hurdle, skipped a beat, got hurt

Enduring the responsibility with a little twinkle,

End it up with acceptance as a pinch of sprinkle!

- Kusum Choudhary

Day 35
For You

A never-ending count of stars,
Blaming the numbers which couldn't
Capture the beautiful scars!

Her laugh sets every bit of bar high,
The scenery of multiverse is owned in her eyes,
Different shades paint each sky.

Goofy her side, bubbly her with a dimple smile,
I gaze at her speak as if it's just the beginning in a while,
Floral aroma she wears fades every flower's scent,
Nature's involvement made her in eternity they spent.

Old and vintage cards with words never discovered,

Sugary words in salt sprinkles, not once recovered

A versifier like me brought'em since I saw you

Made me fall into the illusion of writing endless verse just for you!

- Kusum Choudhary

Day 36
Flow of Wave

Seems to know it's a world of people and pens;
One is against, and other is backbone being invisible,

Roams handling the world inside,
Devote each piece, yet no one's beside,
Some discard their loveful,
Mold its self-life awful.

Stopples gibberish, nameless yells they gave,
A person with a pen built an ocean with a flow of waves.

Speech with high, aim of none,

Their work in corner is always undone,

Learning from eye, touch from mind,

Lives in painted scenes even being blind.

- Kusum Choudhary

Day 37

Ceremony of Shrine

Room with religious partition,

Invocation to one in unlike forms,

Listener he, only magician,

Together gathering among, calms the storm.

For new dawn, headed with flowers gain a blessing fall,

Sweet fades the sour and bitter,

Song of praise that shades rain of glitters,

Again a day, freshness walk to almighty he calls.

Glory of spirit, inner shines,

Aura with scents the water purifies,

Habitat filled with individualities,

Cross-boundary of the shrine,

Opens doors for cleaning with visuality,

Hands in hands oath with the supreme; battle for cruelty!

The life each got, miracles of god he showers,

Birth and end of his children evolve,

Tied his hands, unable to fix,

Yet it's the powers he owns.

- Kusum Choudhary

Day 38

Paint Brush

Being alive to carve a shape in existence,

Choose a brush to make it fine or ruin,

Dye someone's pain with forgiveness,

Coffee, if bitter, sprinkle a snow that brews in.

Imaginary image virtual world part I'm,

Clouds make happy, and rain makes dance,

Stuck self in ways I build, goddamn,

The warning horn rings in advance,

After the blow, just could take a glance.

Shower colors like a rainbow after raindrops,

Glimmer-like droplets on flowers,

Breathe a day, though pain never falls.

Create empty hours with a sweet melody,

Move out as paint like an orange,

Pathways guide certain destiny,

Countless goods Florence.

Create a creative among creatures yet not in a rush,

Life is beautiful, like falling leaf's scents,
Apply like a paintbrush.

- Kusum Choudhary

Day 39
Fallen Stars

Few are chosen, many are left, others are fallen,

Because their hearts were built of cotton,

The disappeared ones are never recalled,

And their remembrance is not so forgotten.

Before wrinkles, a day before worries,

Just like any usual in a hurry,

Away the end line of getting blurry,

Sudden the pathway of getting buried.

Daily site to see,

Kind of sweet, like cherry on a tree,

Refuse to criticism, painstaking like a honey bee,

No match for cruelty, preferred early to free!

- Kusum Choudhary

Day 40
Lost Survivors

Another morning with usual guilt,

Tried and tested without rest,

Unexpected roads turned into life-built-in liability,

Unspoken me, yelling of life only for,
why didn't you give the best?

Habit to believe yet not to accept,

All I had various aspects,

Didn't know what it meant to not expect?

The last days ended in falling hope,

Burning own soul in disrespect;

Leaving time, changing nights,

Couldn't believe, lost even me with the ending fights,

In days of yore, lies were brighter than lights,

At times, couldn't see the truths in lies,

Along unhandy eyesight.

- Kusum Choudhary

Day 41
Foreign Land

Meant to be advanced, for things left behind,

Journey to land, where you are only new,

Life has happened, over and done with, can't be rewind,

Single odd in thousands of even as a mute,

Among deaf balance, nothing just out of the blue.

Soul of nature as a friendly friend,

Dis-concern by people,

Am I too early? Asked the time I spend,

Desire to be warmed, like their child as equal.

Aroma couldn't beat my home's scents,

My sister's cheeky marshmallow to squeeze,

Here, living in homes built for rents,

Another's plan gets one on the third quiz!

- Kusum Choudhary

Day 42
Purified Feet

Self-declared words, holding grudges for one,
Cleansed their feet, is their heart?
Matters disrespect of any, takes for own fun,
Once freshly bloomed flowers are fallen apart.

Cycle of circle, continuous non-reaching points,
Peaks and valleys all one in earn coins,
How it's pure if speech is cursed,
Bruises from their deeds, sinless souls,
Hopes, why it isn't reversed.

Never took ever calm breath,

Glorified their life's getting,

Where's karma of my filling pot?

Holden what? Is this everything I wanted; I'm returning.

- Kusum Choudhary

Day 43
Turn Over to Jan

Autumn played a role; rainy turned sunny,

Enlarge cold generated winter,

Lighting at Christmas, for the last snowman like a bunny,

Next day, book of letters turned empty pages like first introduction, blinking as a reminder.

New inhale of freshly rising sun,

Dare to work 365 days in fun,

Over and complete of a year,

Return of spring again,

Pretty much seems next day, birth for turn over to Jan!

- Kusum Choudhary

Day 44
Melting Snow

Under snow, beside a burb seems rocky roads,

Pouring comfort in snowy cold,

Hold my hand, until the glacier explodes,

Turn a murky blow in a wormy gold.

Find though maybe hard as ice,

Crystal clear like water,

Packing hearts that's from a lovely gust,

I've melted like snow more than thrice,

Grisly realism around, unsympathetic me,
yet all loved in paracosm lust.

A thunder announcing a dare of war,

Game of compromise,
community value that's a world glow

Too good to be present, goodbye before ninety-four,

Burial beneath a melting snow!

- Kusum Choudhary

Day 45
Sunflower

Droopy rays of day spring,

Crystallizing first evolution like a glacier,

Face like a mini safflower worn as a ring,

Unexpectedly, one who gave others?

Acknowledged by a stranger.

Guard to brighten the dimmed,

Vanishing of dusty, adoration of sunny rose,

Ability showers, loyalty screamed,

Made a form to give a funny pose.

Exaggerated love as a rose,

Unrecognized the buried affection a sunflower holds,

Does comfort never got get decompose?

Valued high, yet one ignored knows;

Guardian angel as healthier seed,

Bloomy heart watching bloomed firstly mirasol,

A garden of a farm ruled by sunflowers is all I need!

Can't be owned its royalty charm one surpasses all.

- Kusum Choudhary

After reading these poems daily, you might know the growth it took me to improve through each verse. Understanding life is not important. The way you enjoy being yourself and not disappointing or ruining because your moods weren't exciting.

Poetry is also a highly subjective art form, and what one reader may find beautiful and moving, another may not. This is because poetry often relies on personal interpretation, and the meaning of a poem can be different for each individual reader.

Short and simple yet most disturbing. Some days I could able to write appealing poem/verse. Even I've spent days in chaos building a unique poem.